COOKING WITH KIDS

Recipe Conversions

⅛ teaspoon = 0.6 mL	1 tablespoon = 15 mL	1 cup = 240 mL
¼ teaspoon = 1.2 mL	⅛ cup = 30 mL	1 fluid ounce = 30 mL
½ teaspoon = 2.5 mL	¼ cup = 60 mL	1 ounce = 28 grams
1 teaspoon = 5 mL	½ cup = 120 mL	1 fluid pound = 500 mL
½ tablespoon = 7.5 mL	¾ cup = 175 mL	1 pound = 453 grams

© 2022 by Brianne Grajkowski and Fox Chapel Publishing Company, Inc., 903 Square Street, Mount Joy, PA 17552.

ISBN 978-1-4971-0304-7

Shutterstock photos: used throughout: Aleksandra Novakovic (pot icon), Anterovium (knife icon); pages 8–9: Anterovium (egg slicer icon), GzP_Design (citrus squeezer icon), Aleksandra Novakovic (pastry brush icon, potato masher icon, cookie scoop icon, pan icon, measuring spoons icon, spoon icon, whisk icon, can opener icon, potato peeler icon, cutting board icon, blender icon, mixer icon, carafe icon), Marina Akinina (popsicle mold icon), Plawarn (cookie cutter icon, measuring cup icon, cookie sheet icon, cupcake pan icon, loaf pan icon), Marharyta Kovalenko (cookie cutter icon, baking dish icon, ice tray icon, foil icon, tart pan icon), jekitut (pressure cooker icon), boris farias (personal blender icon), Oleg_kelt (waffle maker icon), Dshnrgc (grill icon, skewers icon), Nadiinko (bamboo mat icon), Aletheia Shade (jar icon), pavlematic (straw icon); page 206: HandmadePictures.

The Cataloging-in-Publication Data is on file with the Library of Congress.

To learn more about the other great books from Fox Chapel Publishing, or to find a retailer near you, call toll-free 800-457-9112 or visit us at *www.FoxChapelPublishing.com*.

We are always looking for talented authors. To submit an idea, please send a brief inquiry to acquisitions@foxchapelpublishing.com.

Printed in China
First printing

COOKING WITH KIDS

FUN, EASY, APPROACHABLE RECIPES TO HELP TEACH KIDS HOW TO COOK

BRIANNE GRAJKOWSKI

FOX CHAPEL
PUBLISHING

Contents

Introduction

Welcome to *Cooking with Kids*! My family and I are so excited that you've picked up this cookbook and are ready to enjoy making food with your young ones.

One of the great things about cooking with your kids is that it can be both fun *and* educational. It teaches them to be creative and explore new flavors. It teaches measurements, math, and science. It helps with reading, as kids learn new words from the recipes and lists of instructions. And when kids learn how to cook for themselves, they are also learning how to care for themselves, which is something all parents want for their children.

With all this in mind, I've put together more than 100 recipes for you to cook with your kids. There are recipes for breakfast, lunch, dinner, dessert, and snacks, and they include a variety of flavors and food groups. Most importantly, the recipes are kid friendly and accomplishable, but they aren't just "kid food." Whether you're making my Best Ever Banana Bread, Caprese Flatbreads, Bacon & Cheddar Burgers, or Tiramisu, you can find something that the whole family can make, eat, and enjoy together, no matter your age.

Cooking Safely

The first thing you'll need to keep in mind when cooking with kids is kitchen safety. I see three components to cooking safely: listening, timing, and supervision.

Listening. I've always told my kids that the first rule of cooking is listening. If they are having a hard time listening, then it isn't the best time for them to cook or help out. I will ask them to sit down at the table until they are ready to move on. I find this to be the most helpful rule while cooking and learning together so that they remain safe.

Timing. The second rule: safe cooking is fun cooking! As a parent, it's your job to know when it's a good time for you and your child to cook together. If you're in a hurry or starving, save your

Just like my son, James, your kids will turn into a chef in no time!

cooking together for another time. You both want to be ready to learn and enjoy your time together.

Supervision. The third rule of safe cooking with your child is knowing when to supervise. The three areas of the kitchen that I think need the most supervision are a) when using a real knife, b) using a stand mixer, and c) using anything with heat. In these areas, I am always with them at their current level of cooking. Once you've watched over them several times, use your best judgment for when you feel your child is ready to use these items without supervision.

To help you gauge which recipes need more supervision, I've included icons for recipes that use sharp blades and recipes that involve heat. These markings are meant to help you as you are choosing which recipes you'd like to try.

 This recipe uses heat.

 This recipe includes chopping, cutting, or slicing.

How to Get Started

It's important to remember that cooking together can have a learning curve. Don't be discouraged if the first few times don't go exactly as planned. Be sure to keep trying until you find a rhythm together. Learning at the start will be the most challenging. Here are some tips and tricks for how to begin.

Start small. A good age to start teaching kids about cooking is when they are 2 to 4 years old, when they can help with easier tasks like pouring ingredients into a bowl and stirring. When my kids were young, I encouraged them to cook with me. One of their favorite cooking tasks was using the pastry brush to "paint" olive oil onto veggies or tomato sauce onto pizza dough.

Be ready for messiness. Kids will make a mess, and it will take longer to cook the dish than if you were cooking on your own. That's okay because, as your child is learning, it is important to remember to have fun!

Try a simple recipe first. Start with the simplest recipes and move on to recipes you both want to try. I've included symbols for each of the recipes to indicate whether they are easy, medium, or hard. The easy recipes have few ingredients and don't generally involve a lot of steps or complicated tasks. The medium and hard recipes are more complicated, but they are still approachable. You may want to wait to try these once you've practiced cooking together, and you may need to provide more supervision for these types of recipes.

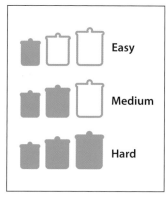

Remind your kids that all the steps they learn will teach them to make delicious food!

Pastry brushes can turn cooking into craft time!

Pre-read the steps. As a parent (or other supervisor), start by pre-reading all the steps of a chosen recipe with your child to make sure you have all the necessary ingredients and equipment and to see if you're ready to accomplish it.

Start with one kid. If you are cooking with more than one child, start one child at a time on a task to make sure he or she is able to focus on what they are learning. Once each child has a good understanding of the steps, you can all cook together.

Lay it all out. We like to gather all the ingredients, tools, dishes, and equipment needed for the recipe and set them out on the counter. We walk through each step together before following the instructions.

Adjust the recipes to your family's tastes. Kids love cooking when there are a lot of colors and familiar ingredients, and when they are making foods they already know and like. If a recipe has an item your child doesn't typically eat, I like to give it a try anyway. Often, when the kids have a hand in making the food, they like to eat it too. If it really becomes a battle, go ahead and modify the recipe with what your child will eat. I love adjusting recipes to fit our family needs, so feel free to do what works and make it fun!

Easy

Medium

Hard

Cooking Tools & Equipment

For the recipes in this book, we tend to use a lot of the same cooking tools again and again, so it's good to have these on hand. I've put together a checklist of the tools we have found most useful when cooking together.

If you don't have the exact tool or piece of equipment called for in a recipe, look around your kitchen to see if you have something that will work. Or, if you decide it's something you will use again, go ahead and purchase it. For example, we use our toaster oven a lot, but if you don't have one, you can always use the oven.

One tool that really put my mind at ease as we began to cook together was a kids' knife set. It made chopping fun and less worrisome for me. We still use these knives when the kids are chopping things that are not too tough. They are both learning to use real knives now and understanding the importance of safety.

A kids' knife set like this one can make chopping easier and safer.

MEASUREMENT ABBREVIATIONS
oz. = ounce
lb./lbs. = pound/pounds
tsp./tsps. = teaspoon/teaspoons
tbsp./tbsps. = tablespoon/tablespoons

TOOLS FOR LITTLE HANDS

☐ Kids' knife set   ☐ Citrus squeezer

☐ Pastry "paint" brush

☐ Egg slicer

☐ Potato masher

☐ 1-inch cookie scoop

☐ Popsicle molds   ☐ Cookie cutters

A citrus squeezer is a fun and easy tool for kids to use.

COMMON KITCHEN TOOLS

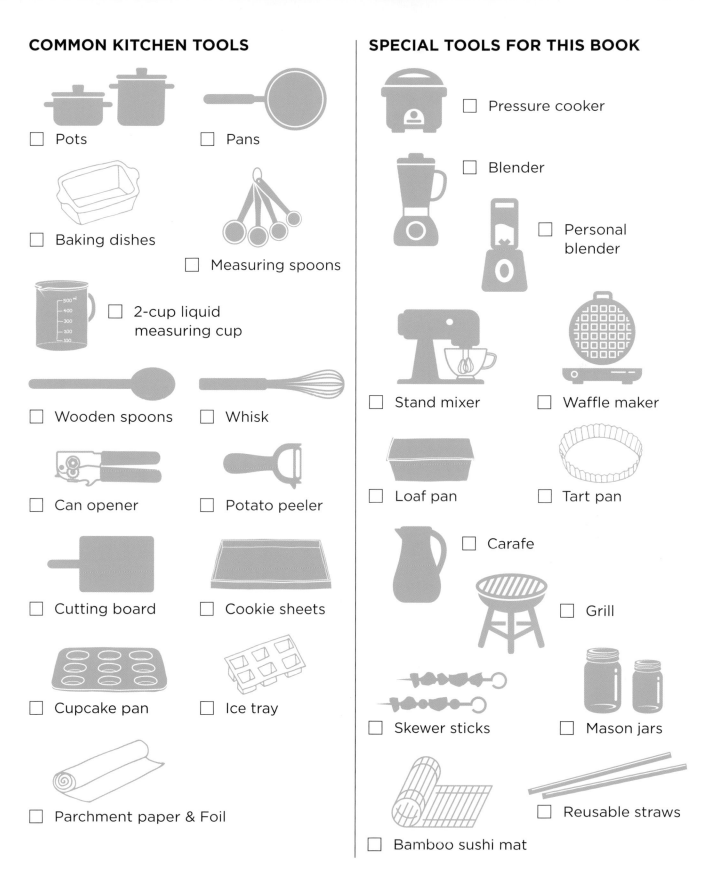

☐ Pots

☐ Pans

☐ Baking dishes

☐ Measuring spoons

☐ 2-cup liquid measuring cup

☐ Wooden spoons

☐ Whisk

☐ Can opener

☐ Potato peeler

☐ Cutting board

☐ Cookie sheets

☐ Cupcake pan

☐ Ice tray

☐ Parchment paper & Foil

SPECIAL TOOLS FOR THIS BOOK

☐ Pressure cooker

☐ Blender

☐ Personal blender

☐ Stand mixer

☐ Waffle maker

☐ Loaf pan

☐ Tart pan

☐ Carafe

☐ Grill

☐ Skewer sticks

☐ Mason jars

☐ Bamboo sushi mat

☐ Reusable straws

All the Fun
DRINKS

Strawberry
LEMONADE

Serves 4-5 | 15 Minutes

INGREDIENTS

1 cup granulated sugar

5½ cups water

2 cups strawberries

4 large lemons

Ice

INSTRUCTIONS

1. Make simple syrup: Add sugar and 1 cup of water to a medium saucepan on medium heat. Stir until combined and the sugar has dissolved.
2. Make strawberry puree: add strawberries and ½ cup water to blender and blend until combined.
3. Squeeze lemons with a lemon press to make lemon juice.
4. Combine simple syrup, strawberry puree, and lemon juice in a pitcher. Add 4 cups of water and stir.
5. Fill glasses with ice, pour strawberry lemonade on top, and serve!

SQUEEZE!
Grab your lemon press and squeeze those lemons!

Wild Blueberry
SMOOTHIE

Serves 1 | 10 Minutes

INGREDIENTS

½ cup frozen wild blueberries

3-4 strawberries

1 cup spinach

1 banana

½ cup water

INSTRUCTIONS

1. Add all ingredients to personal blender cup. Attach blade lid.
2. Push down and blend until all ingredients are combined, about 30 seconds to 1 minute.
3. Pour into glass, garnish with strawberry if desired, and enjoy!

PUSH + BLEND!
Hold down the personal blender until all ingredients combine smoothly!

Pineapple
WHIP

INGREDIENTS

One 15-oz. can coconut milk

2 pineapples cut in chunks and frozen, or one 16-oz. bag frozen pineapples

INSTRUCTIONS

1. Open coconut milk with can opener and stir.
2. Pour coconut milk and frozen pineapple chunks into a blender.
3. Blend until combined, adding water if needed. Serve right away and enjoy!

TWIST!
Once the can opener is attached to the can, twist the handle until it moves all the way around the can.

Green Apple
SODA

Serves 6 | 20 Minutes

INGREDIENTS

½ cup granulated sugar

1 green apple, peeled, sliced, and cored

½ cup water

Lime soda water

INSTRUCTIONS

1. Add the sugar, green apple peels and core, and water to a small saucepan and heat on medium until boiling.
2. Reduce heat to low and simmer for 5 minutes.
3. Remove the apple sweetener from heat and let sit for 10 minutes.
4. Pour through a strainer into a glass.
5. Add ice to glasses and pour 1 tablespoon of apple sweetener to each glass. Top with lime soda water.

SIMMER!
Simmer the apple core and peels together with sugar and water to make an apple sweetener!

Orange FLOAT

Serves 1 | 5 Minutes

INGREDIENTS

- 1 scoop vanilla bean ice cream
- ½ cup orange juice
- 1 orange slice
- Mint for garnish

INSTRUCTIONS

1. Place a scoop of ice cream into a glass.
2. Pour orange juice on top.
3. Cut a slice in the middle of the orange slice and hang on rim of the glass.
4. Add a sprig of mint on top of the ice cream to garnish.

SCOOP!
Use a large ice cream scoop to get the ice cream out of the container and into a glass!

Blackberry
SMOOTHIE

Serves 1 | 5 Minutes

INGREDIENTS

½ cup blackberries

½ cup blueberries

1 banana

½ cup strawberry yogurt

1 cup spinach

½ cup water

3 ice cubes (if using fresh fruit)

INSTRUCTIONS

1. Rinse berries.
2. Add all ingredients to a blender.
3. Pulse to mix and blend until smooth.
4. Garnish with fresh berries if desired.

MEASURE!
Use a measuring cup to measure ingredients. It's okay if the ingredients "heap" over the top—smoothie measurements don't have to be exact!

Mango-Coconut
SMOOTHIE

Serves 1 | 5 Minutes

INGREDIENTS

1 mango

1 frozen banana, chopped

1 tbsp. coconut milk

2 tbsps. water

INSTRUCTIONS

1. Cut the skin of the mango off. Then slice into pieces, cutting around the inner pit.
2. Add all items to a blender and blend for 1 minute until smooth.
3. Pour and serve!

SLICE!
Hold the mango up and slice down around the inner pit. Don't cut into the pit. The fruit is the soft part under the skin.

LIMEONADE

Serves 6 | 10 Minutes

INGREDIENTS

½ cup granulated sugar

6 cups water

6 lemons

3 limes

Ice

INSTRUCTIONS

1. Make simple syrup: add sugar and 2 cups water to a medium saucepan and heat until sugar dissolves, about 4 minutes.
2. Use a handheld juicer to squeeze the juice out of limes and lemons.
3. Pour 1 ½ cups of the simple syrup and the juice into large pitcher. Fill with 4 cups of water.
4. Add more simple syrup to taste.
5. Add ice to glasses and fill with limeonade. Serve!

SAVE IT!
Save any remaining simple syrup in the fridge. You can add it to soda water, popsicles, or tea!

Pomegranate
FIZZ

Serves 4 | 5 Minutes

INGREDIENTS

1 pomegranate

2 limes, juiced

Ice

1 liter ginger ale

Rosemary for garnish

INSTRUCTIONS

1. To remove seeds from pomegranate, start by cutting a circle around the crown to pop it off. Then make slices down the white vein and pull slices open.
2. Fill a bowl with water, peel seeds away from the membrane, and drop the seeds into the water.
3. Any remaining membrane will float to the top. Remove the membrane and strain the seeds to remove the water.
4. Use a juice squeezer to make pomegranate juice. Add about a tablespoon of seeds one at a time to the juicer to squeeze. Repeat until all seeds are juiced.
5. Set out 4 glasses. To each glass, add a handful of ice, 1 cup ginger ale, 2 tablespoons pomegranate juice, and 1 teaspoon lime juice.
6. Garnish each glass with a slice of lime and a sprig of rosemary.

GARNISH!
Adding a garnish is optional, but it makes drinks fun for special occasions.

Breakfast
IS READY

Best Ever
BANANA BREAD

Serves 6 | 1 Hour and 10 Minutes

INGREDIENTS

1 tbsp. butter, room temperature

¾ cup granulated sugar

1 egg

¼ cup butter, melted

3 ripe bananas

1 tsp. salt

1 tsp. baking soda

1½ cups flour

INSTRUCTIONS

1. Preheat oven to 325°F.
2. Grease a 9 × 5-inch loaf pan with room-temperature butter.
3. In a bowl, mash together sugar, egg, melted butter, and bananas.
4. In a small dish, mix salt and baking soda together, then stir into banana mixture.
5. Add flour and stir until batter is combined.
6. Pour into loaf pan and bake for 50 minutes to 1 hour or until a toothpick comes out clean.

MASH!
Mash the bananas using a masher or fork!

Strawberry & Nutella
PANCAKES

Serves 4–6 | 20 Minutes

INGREDIENTS

- 1 tbsp. granulated sugar
- 3 tsps. baking powder
- 1 tsp. salt
- 1½ cups flour
- 1¼ cups milk
- 3 tbsps. melted butter
- 1 egg
- Half 7.7-oz. jar Nutella
- 10 strawberries, sliced
- Powdered sugar, shaved almonds, and mini chocolate chips for toppings

INSTRUCTIONS

1. Mix the granulated sugar, baking powder, salt, and flour in a bowl.
2. Add in the milk, butter, and egg and stir until combined into a batter. If you let the batter sit for a few minutes, it makes the pancakes even fluffier.
3. Heat a skillet on medium heat. Butter the pan.
4. Use a ½-cup measuring cup to pour the pancake batter into the pan.
5. Wait until there are bubbles all through the pancakes before flipping.
6. Cook an additional 1 to 2 minutes on the second side.
7. Spread Nutella on top of pancakes. Top with sliced strawberries, powdered sugar, shaved almonds, and mini chocolate chips. Serve!

DECORATE!
Decorate your pancake with toppings to your liking!

Scrambled
EGG BAR

Serves 4-6 | 15 Minutes

INGREDIENTS

- 6-8 eggs
- 1 tbsp. olive oil
- 1 cup shredded cheddar cheese
- 1 cup cherry tomatoes, sliced in halves
- 1 cup cooked potatoes O'Brien or other cooked potatoes of choice
- 1 cup cooked diced ham
- 1 cup cooked breakfast sausage crumbles
- 2 tbsps. sour cream
- 4-6 toasted English muffins

INSTRUCTIONS

1. Scramble the eggs: Crack eggs into a 2-cup liquid measuring cup and stir to combine. Add olive oil to a medium skillet on medium heat. Pour eggs into the skillet and let cook for about 5 to 7 minutes, stirring occasionally.
2. Add scrambled eggs to large bowl and set aside.
3. Add remaining items to separate bowls.
4. Set out plates and forks for your scrambled egg bar.
5. Each person can make their own plate with whichever toppings they love most.

TOP IT UP!
Use a fork to grab toppings for your scrambled eggs!

Egg + Avo
TOAST

Serves 4 | 10 minutes

INGREDIENTS

2 avocados

4 hard-boiled eggs

4 pieces bread

2 tbsps. mayo

1 tbsp. everything bagel seasoning

INSTRUCTIONS

1. Slice avocados in half. Then use a spoon to scoop out avocado. Slice into thin slices.
2. Use an egg slicer or knife to slice eggs thin.
3. Add bread to toaster and toast lightly.
4. Spread mayo on the toast.
5. Top with sliced avocado, then sliced egg. Sprinkle seasoning on top.

SLICE!
Use an egg slicer to slice eggs thin!

Fresh Start Yogurt & BERRIES

Serves 4 | 15 Minutes

INGREDIENTS

1 cup strawberries

1 cup blueberries

1 cup blackberries

1 cup granola

2 tbsps. honey

One 32-oz. container yogurt

INSTRUCTIONS

1. Add all berries to colander. Rinse with water and drain.
2. Cut the stems off the strawberries and slice.
3. Arrange all berries on serving dish.
4. Place granola in a small bowl. Place honey in a small dish.
5. Get out four bowls. Add 1 cup of yogurt to each bowl.
6. Sprinkle the granola onto the yogurt.
7. Add berries of your choice to each bowl.
8. Drizzle with honey and serve.

DRIZZLE!
Use a honey wand or a spoon to drizzle honey into your yogurt bowl.

Hawaiian
WAFFLES

Serves 6 | 15 Minutes

INGREDIENTS

2 cups flour

1 tbsp. granulated sugar

1 tbsp. baking powder

¼ tsp. salt

1½ cups milk

½ cup melted butter

2 eggs

½ tsp. vanilla

1 cup chopped pineapple

2 bananas, sliced

1 tbsp. coconut flakes

Use extra caution with a waffle iron because once you plug it in, the whole unit will get hot. Use an oven mitt to open the waffle iron.

INSTRUCTIONS

1. Add flour, sugar, baking powder, and salt to a bowl and stir.
2. Add milk, butter, eggs, and vanilla to the dry mixture and stir to combine.
3. Add ½ cup of batter to a waffle maker and cook on medium heat until cooked.
4. Repeat until all batter is made into waffles.
5. Top waffles with pineapple, bananas, and coconut flakes and serve.

POUR!
Make sure the waffle iron is turned on and ready before pouring the batter into the center of the waffle maker!

Chocolate Chip SCONES

Serves 5 | 30 Minutes

INGREDIENTS

- Cooking spray
- ¾ cup half-and-half
- ¼ cup granulated sugar
- 2 tsps. vanilla extract
- 1 large egg

- 2½ cups all-purpose flour + more for kneading
- 1 tbsp. baking powder
- ½ tsp. salt

- 3 tbsps. butter, chilled and cut into small pieces
- ¾ cup chocolate chips
- 1 large egg white
- 1½ tbsps. granulated sugar for topping

INSTRUCTIONS

1. Preheat oven to 375°F.
2. Spray baking sheet with cooking spray or brush with olive oil.
3. Combine the half-and-half, sugar, vanilla, and egg in a medium bowl, stirring with a whisk.
4. Combine flour, baking powder, and salt in a large bowl, stirring with a whisk.
5. Cut chilled butter into flour mixture using a fork. Mix butter in well with your hands.
6. Add the cream mixture, stirring just until moist.
7. Gently fold in chocolate chips.
8. Place dough onto a floured surface and knead lightly four times with floured hands.
9. On a baking sheet, form dough into a 9-inch circle about ¾-inch thick. Using a knife, cut the dough into 8 wedges, all the way through.
10. Brush egg white on all 8 pieces and sprinkle with sugar.
11. Bake for 20 minutes or until golden on the edges.

MIX IT UP!

Use different kinds of chips, like white chocolate, dark chocolate, or peanut butter, for a variety of flavors!

Orange Cream
FRENCH TOAST

Serves 4–6 | 20 Minutes

INGREDIENTS

- 4 eggs
- 1 cup half-and-half
- 2 tbsps. orange zest
- 1½ oranges, squeezed
- 1 tsp. cinnamon
- 1 tsp. nutmeg
- 8 slices thick bread
- ½ stick butter
- ½ cup whipping cream
- Orange slices for garnish

INSTRUCTIONS

1. Add eggs, half-and-half, 1 tablespoon orange zest, one-third of the orange juice, cinnamon, and nutmeg to a shallow dish and stir until combined.
2. Dip each slice of bread into the mixture and soak on both sides. Add to plate and set aside.
3. Heat butter in a medium skillet on medium heat.
4. Add 2 slices of soaked bread to the skillet and cook for 2 to 3 minutes per side. Repeat for the remainder of the slices.
5. Place remaining orange zest, whipping cream, and remaining orange juice in a blender and blend for 30 seconds to 1 minute to create orange whipping cream.
6. Top French toast with orange whipping cream and serve with orange slices.

DIP!
Using your fingers, dip each slice of bread into the mixture and soak on both sides!

Sausage & Egg
ENGLISH MUFFINS

Serves 4 | 10 Minutes

INGREDIENTS

- 6 eggs
- 1 tbsp. butter
- 4 slices cheddar cheese
- 4 English muffins
- 4 slices cooked breakfast sausage
- 2 tbsps. mayo

INSTRUCTIONS

1. Crack eggs into a liquid measuring cup and stir with a fork until combined.
2. Heat butter in a skillet on medium heat.
3. Pour eggs into the skillet to cook through, stirring occasionally.
4. Add sliced cheese to eggs to melt cheese.
5. Use a spatula to cut the eggs into four pieces.
6. Toast English muffins and heat sausages in microwave for 1 minute.
7. Use a butter knife to add mayo to the bottom English muffin. Add sausage.
8. Use the spatula to scoop the egg and cheese onto the sausage.
9. Top with the English muffin top.

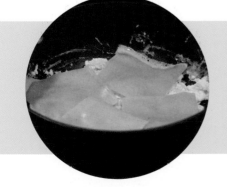

MELT!
Add cheese evenly to the top of the cooked eggs so the cheese will melt into the eggs.

Make-Ahead Breakfast
BURRITOS

Serves 8 | 25 Minutes

INGREDIENTS

One 16-oz. package bacon

12 eggs

1 tbsp. olive oil

2 cups shredded cheese

8 tortillas

Salsa (optional)

INSTRUCTIONS

1. Preheat oven to 400°F.
2. Set out bacon in a single layer on baking sheet. Cook for 15 minutes.
3. Crack eggs into large bowl and stir.
4. Add olive oil to a medium skillet and heat on medium.
5. Add eggs and cook 5 to 7 minutes until cooked through, stirring occasionally.
6. Add eggs, 1 slice bacon, and a sprinkle of cheese to each tortilla.
7. Roll tortillas into burritos.
8. Enjoy right away or store in ziplock bag in the fridge for up to 4 days for make-ahead burritos.

ROLLIN'!
To roll a burrito, fold the right and left side of the tortilla toward the center. Take front of the tortilla and roll toward the back.

Brown Sugar
OATS

Serves 4 | 5 Minutes

INGREDIENTS

¼ tsp. salt

3½ cups water

2 cups instant oats

1 tbsp. brown sugar

Butter, cream, bananas, mangos (optional)

INSTRUCTIONS

1. Add salt, water, and oats to a medium saucepan on medium heat. Bring to a boil and cook for 1 minute.
2. Cut up any fruit, if desired.
3. Add brown sugar to oats and stir until mixed. Scoop oats mixture into four bowls.
4. Top with butter, cream, bananas, and/or mangos as desired, and serve.

PREP!
While your oats are coming to a boil, cut up any fruit or toppings you'd like to add.

Oatmeal
BAKE

INGREDIENTS

1 cup butter, melted

2 eggs

1 cup brown sugar

2 tsps. vanilla

½ tsp. salt

1 tsp. baking soda

1 tsp. baking powder

1½ cups flour

2 cups oats

1 cup chocolate chips

INSTRUCTIONS

1. Preheat oven to 350°F.
2. Lightly grease an 8 × 8-inch dish with butter.
3. Crack eggs into bowl and stir.
4. Add in sugar, vanilla, and butter and stir until combined.
5. In a separate bowl, combine salt, baking soda, baking powder, flour, and oats.
6. Pour eggs mixture into dry ingredients bowl and stir to combine.
7. Add in chocolate chips.
8. Pour into dish and bake for 30 minutes.

STIR!
Make sure to stir the eggs well to mix the whites and the yolks!

Tot
CASSEROLE

Serves 6–8 | 55 Minutes

INGREDIENTS

6 eggs

One 32-oz. bag tater tots

½ cup milk

1 tsp. salt

½ tsp. ground mustard

1 lb. breakfast sausage, cooked

1 cup cheese

Cilantro for garnish

INSTRUCTIONS

1. Preheat oven to 350°F.
2. Crack eggs into a bowl and stir.
3. Pour tater tots into a 13 × 9-inch baking dish.
4. Pour eggs, milk, and seasonings onto tots and stir.
5. Add sausage and cheese.
6. Bake for 45 minutes or until egg is cooked through.
7. Garnish with chopped cilantro.

PREP!
Grab all your ingredients together before you start cooking!

Spam +
EGGS

INGREDIENTS

1 can Spam

8 eggs

INSTRUCTIONS

1. Open can of Spam and slice into ¼-inch squares: Slice lengthwise, then turn and slice again. Flip and slice one more time until you have squares or small pieces of Spam.
2. Crack eggs into a 2-cup liquid measuring cup and stir with a fork until combined.
3. Cook Spam in a medium pan on medium heat until browned.
4. Pour eggs over spam and heat until eggs are cooked through, about 4 minutes.

WHISK!
Stir fork quickly to cause the eggs to swirl. Mix the yolks and whites together.

Lunchtime Is the
BEST TIME

Ham & Cheese
SLIDERS

Serves 4 | 15 Minutes

INGREDIENTS

One 12-oz. package brioche rolls or Hawaiian rolls

One 8-oz. package sliced cheddar cheese

One 12-oz. package ham

¼ cup butter

1 tbsp. everything bagel seasoning

INSTRUCTIONS

1. Cut brioche buns or Hawaiian rolls in half.
2. On bottom halves of buns, add slices of cheddar cheese and cooked ham to layer cheese, ham, then cheese again. Put the bun or slider tops back on top.
3. Spread melted butter on top with your kitchen brush.
4. Sprinkle with seasoning.
5. Bake or toast at 350°F for 3 to 5 minutes or until the cheese is melted.

LAYER!
Two layers of cheese makes for extra-cheesy sliders!

Pepperoni & Bacon
PIZZA

Serves 4–8 | 30 Minutes

INGREDIENTS

2 cups whole wheat flour

2 cups white flour

2¼ tsps. instant dry yeast

1 tsp. granulated sugar

2 tsps. salt

3-4 tbsps. olive oil

1½ cups water

1 cup pizza or pasta sauce

1 cup mozzarella
shredded cheese

½ cup pepperoni

½ cup cooked bacon

INSTRUCTIONS

1. Preheat oven to 400°F.
2. Put flour, yeast, sugar, and salt in a mixer and start the mixer on low.
3. Slowly add 2 tablespoons olive oil and the water. Mix until combined.
4. Add flour to a work surface.
5. Knead the dough three times. Cut in half to make two pizza doughs. One pizza dough can be frozen to be used another time.
6. Cover the dough in plastic wrap and let rise for 1 hour.
7. Spread 1 to 2 tablespoons olive oil on a pizza pan.
8. Knead the dough two times and roll out.
9. Paint on the sauce, then sprinkle the cheese and toppings on top.
10. Bake for 13 to 15 minutes.

PAINT & SPRINKLE!
Paint on your pizza sauce and sprinkle your toppings on top!

Tomato
SOUP

Serves 4 | 50 Minutes

INGREDIENTS

½ onion

4 tbsps. olive oil

1 tbsp. chopped garlic

One 28-oz. can tomatoes

2 cups chicken broth

½ tsp. salt

1 cup chopped basil

INSTRUCTIONS

1. Cut onion into ½-inch chunks.
2. Sauté onion in olive oil for 2 minutes in a large stockpot.
3. Add garlic and cook for 1 minute.
4. Add tomatoes, chicken broth, and salt and bring to a boil.
5. Reduce heat and simmer for 35 minutes on medium to low heat.
6. Add basil and cook for 5 minutes. Remove from heat.
7. Use an immersion blender on low to pulse ingredients together.

Adults should use the immersion blender to blend the soup because it will be hot. You can also use a blender or food processor for this step.

IMMERSE!
Make sure to keep the blade of your immersion blender submerged in the soup while pulsing the ingredients together! Another option is to pour the soup into a blender or food processor to blend.

Turkey
ROLL-UPS ⊘

Serves 4 | 10 Minutes

INGREDIENTS

One 12-oz. package turkey lunch meat

2 pieces romaine lettuce

One 8-oz. package cream cheese

½ cup shredded cheddar cheese

One 2.25-oz. can sliced olives

4 tortillas

INSTRUCTIONS

1. Chop up turkey and romaine lettuce into ¼-inch pieces.
2. Add cream cheese, lettuce, turkey, cheese, and olives into a mixing bowl and stir until combined.
3. Spread ¼ cup of the mixture onto tortilla and roll up. Repeat for all rolls and serve.

SPREAD!
Use the back of the measuring cup to help spread out the mixture.

Ground Beef
TACOS

Serves 4 | 20 Minutes

INGREDIENTS

- 1 lb. ground beef
- 3 tbsps. taco seasoning
- One 15-oz. can traditional refried beans
- One 12.6-oz. box crunchy taco shells
- 1 cup lettuce, shredded
- ½ cup tomatoes, chopped
- 1 bunch cilantro, chopped
- 1 avocado, sliced
- ¼ cup cotija or crumbled cheese
- ½ cup sour cream

INSTRUCTIONS

1. Heat ground beef in a skillet on medium heat until cooked.
2. Add taco seasoning and ½ cup of water and simmer on low heat for 5 minutes.
3. Heat up refried beans in saucepan for about 5 minutes.
4. Warm taco shells in the microwave for 30 seconds.
5. Add a layer of refried beans and ground beef to each taco shell.
6. Top tacos with lettuce, tomatoes, cilantro, avocado, cotija cheese, and sour cream as desired.

DRIZZLE!

Add sour cream to a plastic sandwich bag and cut a hole in the corner. Squeeze the bag to drizzle sour cream over the tacos. Add a teaspoon of hot sauce to the sour cream if you want a little spice.

Best Chef's
SALAD 🔪

Serves 4 | 15 Minutes

INGREDIENTS

1 head romaine lettuce

1 cucumber

Two 8-oz. packages sliced cheese, like sharp cheddar or provolone

One 12-oz. package sliced ham

15 cherry tomatoes

1 bag baby carrots

1 bag croutons

4 hard-boiled eggs

½ cup ranch dressing

INSTRUCTIONS

1. Chop lettuce and slice cucumber, cheeses, and ham.
2. Arrange lettuce in bowls or lunch containers. Top with cucumber, cheese, ham, tomatoes, carrots, and croutons.
3. Slice eggs with egg slicer and add to salad. Serve with a side of ranch dressing. Best Chef's Salads make for a great on-the-go meal!

SLICE!
Peel your hard-boiled eggs and place them one at a time into the egg slicer. Push closed to slice each egg.

Egg & Ham
BAGUETTES

Serves 6 | 15 Minutes

INGREDIENTS

1 tbsp. butter

4 eggs

1 large or 2 small baguettes, sliced in half lengthwise

8 slices Black Forest ham

4 slices white cheddar cheese

Salt and pepper, to taste

1 cup arugula

1 avocado, sliced

1 red onion, sliced thin

2 tbsps. honey mustard dressing

INSTRUCTIONS

1. Heat a medium skillet on medium heat for 3 minutes.
2. Add butter to pan and crack eggs into pan once butter is melted. Cook for 1 to 2 minutes or until whites are almost cooked. Flip eggs and cook 30 more seconds.
3. Toast the baguette, with the ham and cheese on the bottom half. Toast in a toaster over for 350°F for about 5 to 7 minutes or until cheese has melted.
4. Top with eggs and add salt and pepper.
5. Add arugula, avocado, and red onions to the top of the baguette.
6. Drizzle honey mustard dressing over the eggs.
7. Slice into the size you'd like and enjoy!

OVER EASY!
Cook eggs until the whites are almost cooked, then, using a rubber spatula, flip and cook for 30 seconds more.

Salami
GRILLED CHEESE

Serves 4 | 10 Minutes

INGREDIENTS

2 tbsps. butter

One 20-oz. loaf artisan white bread

One 8-oz. package salami

One 8-oz. package cheddar cheese

INSTRUCTIONS

1. Spread butter on one side of the bread, two pieces for each sandwich.
2. Add bread, butter side down, to a griddle pan on medium heat. Place 3 slices of salami then cheese on top of the bread.
3. Top with another slice of buttered bread, butter side up.
4. Grill about 2 minutes, then flip. Grill another minute, or until golden brown. Repeat for remaining sandwiches.

GRIDDLE!
Use a griddle pan to make fun grill marks!

Meatball
SAMMIES

Serves 4 | 15 Minutes

INGREDIENTS

One 20-oz. package cooked frozen meatballs

One 12-oz. package dinner rolls or Hawaiian rolls

1 cup tomato sauce

1 cup shredded mozzarella cheese

1 tbsp. butter, melted

1 tbsp. Parmesan cheese

INSTRUCTIONS

1. Preheat toaster oven or conventional oven to 350°F and cook meatballs according to package instructions.
2. Slice rolls in half lengthwise and top with one meatball per roll.
3. Spread tomato sauce on top.
4. Sprinkle with mozzarella.
5. Cover with tops of rolls and coat with butter.
6. Sprinkle on Parmesan cheese.
7. Bake for 5 to 7 minutes or until cheese is melted.

COOK!
Make sure to cook or heat the meatballs before making the sammies!

Sub
SAMMIES

Serves 4–6 | 10 Minutes

INGREDIENTS

One 12-oz. package sub sandwich rolls

One 8-oz. package sliced turkey deli meat

One 8-oz. package salami

One 8-oz. package pepperoni

One 8-oz. package sliced sharp cheddar cheese

1 tbsp. red wine vinegar

1 tbsp. olive oil

1 tsp. ground mustard

Salt and pepper, to taste

3 tomatoes

1 head romaine lettuce

One 2.25-oz. can sliced black olives

INSTRUCTIONS

1. Slice sub sandwich rolls in half lengthwise.
2. Top with sliced turkey, salami, pepperoni, and cheese.
3. Toast in toaster oven at 350°F for about 5 minutes or until cheese has melted. While sandwich is toasting, whisk vinegar, olive oil, mustard, salt, and pepper in a mixing bowl to combine.
4. Top sub sandwich with tomatoes, lettuce, and olives. Pour the dressing on top and serve.

SLICE!
Use a bread knife. Bread knives are serrated, which means they have a jagged edge like a saw. Ask an adult to supervise, and take your time!

Creamy
TUNA

Serves 2 | 10 Minutes

INGREDIENTS

One 5-oz. can tuna

4 oz. cream cheese

1 tsp. Dijon mustard

1 tbsp. fresh dill, chopped, for garnish

INSTRUCTIONS

1. Add all ingredients to a mixing bowl and stir to combine.
2. Sprinkle with dill for garnish.

CHOP!
Slice dill off the stem and chop into smaller pieces.

Caprese
FLATBREADS

Serves 4 | 20 Minutes

INGREDIENTS

2 tbsps. olive oil

1 package naan tandoori
or flatbread (4 slices)

1 cup shredded mozzarella cheese

3 Kumato or Roma tomatoes, sliced

Salt

Basil leaves

INSTRUCTIONS

1. Preheat toaster oven to 350°F.
2. Brush olive oil onto naan and sprinkle with cheese.
3. Top with 3 to 4 sliced tomatoes. Sprinkle tomatoes with salt.
4. Bake for 5 to 7 minutes.
5. Top with fresh basil. Repeat for each naan.

BRUSH!
Use a kitchen brush to coat
each slice of naan with olive oil.

Feta Greek
SALAD

Serves 4 | 10 Minutes

INGREDIENTS

- 1 tsp. minced garlic
- 1 tsp. Dijon mustard
- 1 tbsp. red wine vinegar
- 1 tbsp. olive oil
- ¼ tsp. salt and pepper

- 1 English cucumber
- 5 vine-ripe tomatoes
- ½ cup feta cheese
- ¼ cup diced black olives

INSTRUCTIONS

1. To make the dressing, whisk garlic, mustard, vinegar, olive oil, salt, and pepper in a bowl until combined.
2. Cut cucumber in half lengthwise, then chop into ¼-inch pieces.
3. Cut tomatoes in half, then slice into pieces.
4. Chop feta into ¼-inch pieces.
5. Pour all ingredients into a glass dish and stir to combine.

WHISK!
Stir quickly to combine the dressing!

Chicken Noodle
SOUP

Serves 6 | 55 Minutes

INGREDIENTS

- 1 onion, diced
- 3 carrots, peeled and diced
- 3 celery, diced
- 2 tbsps. olive oil
- 1 tbsp. minced garlic
- 8 cups chicken stock
- 2 bay leaves
- ¼ tsp. dried thyme
- Salt and pepper
- 2 boneless skinless chicken breasts
- One 12-oz. package egg noodles
- 1 tbsp. dill, chopped, for garnish
- 1 tbsp. lemon juice

INSTRUCTIONS

1. Add onion, carrots, celery, and olive oil to a large stockpot and cook on medium heat for 5 minutes.
2. Add garlic and cook for 1 minute.
3. Add stock, seasonings, and chicken and boil for 35 minutes.
4. Remove chicken and dice into ½-inch pieces.
5. Stir in chicken and noodles and cook for 7 to 10 minutes until noodles are cooked.
6. Add dill and lemon and serve.

DICE!
Dice all your veggies into ¼-inch pieces so they cook down well for your soup!

Jicama Mango
SALAD 🔪

Serves 4 | 15 Minutes

INGREDIENTS

- 2 mangos
- 1 small jicama
- 1 bunch mint
- 1 lime

INSTRUCTIONS

1. Cut mango into thin slices.
2. Cut skin off of jicama and cut into thin slices.
3. Chop mint.
4. Place mango and jicama slices on a plate and squeeze lime juice over slices.
5. Garnish with mint and serve.

SLICE THIN!
For optimal taste, cut the fruit into long, thin slices!

Snacks & Sides
FOR THE WIN

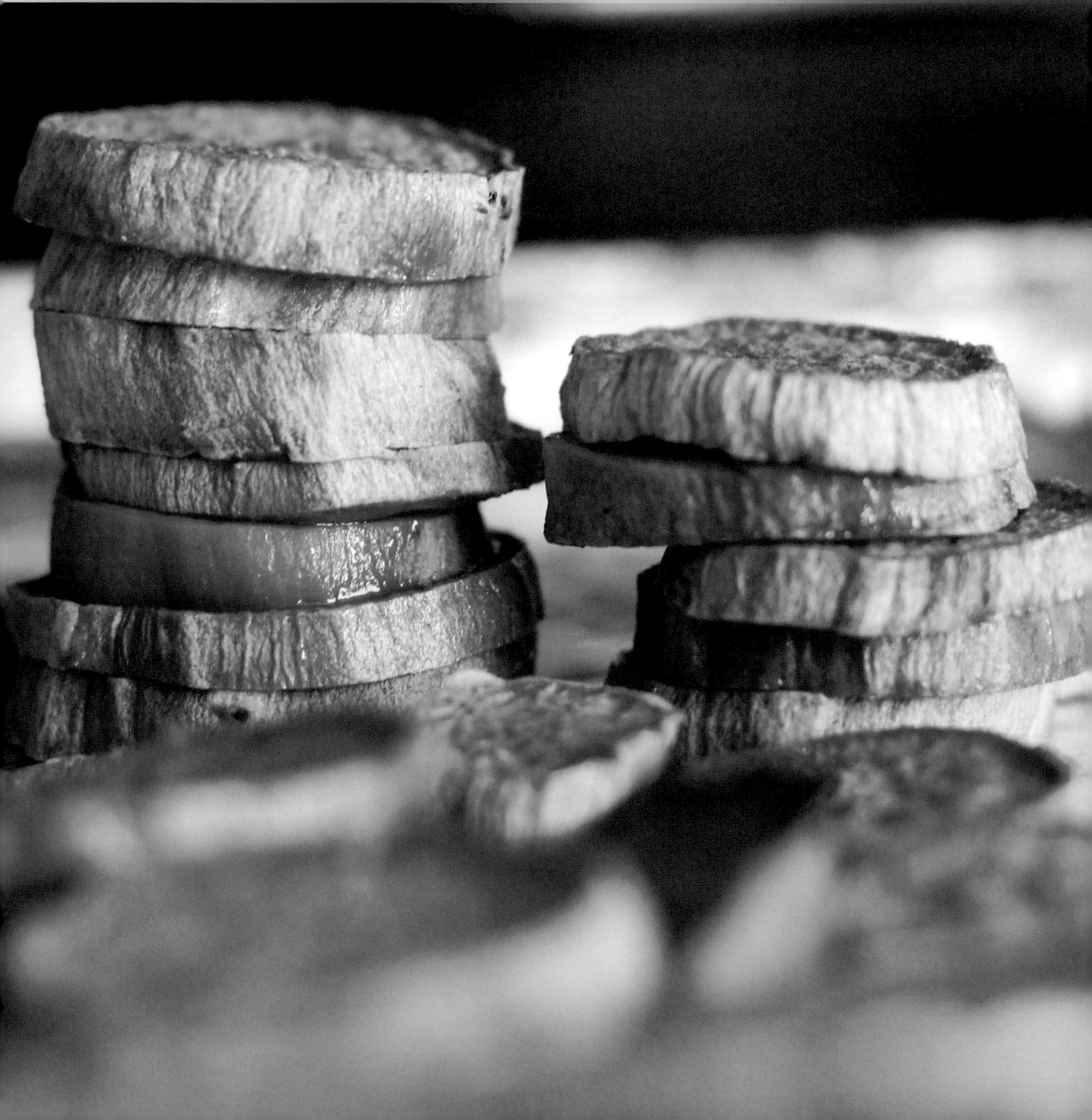

Sweet Potato
BITES

Serves 4 | 30 Minutes

INGREDIENTS

1 sweet potato or yam

2 tbsps. olive oil

1 tsp. salt

INSTRUCTIONS

1. Preheat oven to 375°F.
2. Use a potato peeler to peel the sweet potato.
   Dice potato into ¼-inch-thick slices.
3. Spread out onto a foil- or parchment-lined cookie sheet.
4. Use a basting brush to paint the oil onto the potatoes.
5. Sprinkle with salt.
6. Bake for 20 minutes or until golden on the edges.

PAINT!
Make sure to get oil on the top and bottom of the sweet potato bites.

Fresh Dill
PICKLES

Serves 4 | 20 Minutes

INGREDIENTS

1 cup white vinegar

1 cup water

1 tbsp. salt

2 tbsps. granulated sugar

½ tbsp. peppercorns

1 tbsp. minced garlic

2 tbsps. chopped dill

2–4 small cucumbers, quartered

INSTRUCTIONS

1. Boil vinegar, water, salt, sugar, and peppercorns until combined, about 5 minutes.
2. Add garlic, dill, and cucumbers to a canning jar.
3. Pour vinegar mixture over cucumbers.
4. Refrigerate to let cool.

ADD!
Add garlic for more flavor in your pickles!

Kale
CHIPS

Serves 4 | 10 Minutes

INGREDIENTS

1 bunch kale

2 tbsps. olive oil

1 tsp. salt

INSTRUCTIONS

1. Preheat oven to 375°F.
2. Spread out kale on a foil- or parchment-lined cookie sheet.
3. Use a basting brush to paint the oil onto the kale.
4. Sprinkle with salt.
5. Bake for 5 to 7 minutes or until golden on the edges.

SPRINKLE!
Use your thumb and index finger to pinch the salt and sprinkle it on the kale.

PB Banana
BITES

Serves 1-2 | 5 Minutes

INGREDIENTS

1 banana

Peanut butter

Honey

Mini chocolate chips

Coconut flakes

INSTRUCTIONS

1. Slice banana into ½-inch pieces and spread out onto a plate.
2. Use two small spoons to add a dollop of peanut butter to each banana piece.
3. Drip a few drops of honey on the tops of the peanut butter dollops.
4. Sprinkle a few mini chocolate chips over each bite.
5. Sprinkle on coconut flakes to finish.

SPRINKLE!
Sprinkle on mini chocolate chips and coconut flakes to your liking!

Snack
BOARD

Serves 2 | 10 Minutes

INGREDIENTS

1 orange

1 package white cheddar cheese

1 bunch grapes

1 package pepperoni

1 handful cashews

INSTRUCTIONS

1. Rinse grapes under cool water.
2. Cut orange in half and slice into wedges.
3. Slice cheese into wedges or slices.
4. Arrange all ingredients on a small cutting board and enjoy!

SLICE!
Slice the orange five times to make wedges.

Fruit
CUPS

Serves 4 | 10 minutes

INGREDIENTS

1 orange

1 apple

1 pear

One 1-lb. package strawberries

1 bunch grapes

One 6-oz. package blackberries

One 6-oz. package raspberries

INSTRUCTIONS

1. Rinse fruit with water.
2. Slice orange, apple, and pear into thin slices.
3. Slice stems off strawberries.
4. Set out 4 equal-size cups or bowls.
5. Add a handful of grapes into each dish.
6. Add orange, apple, and pear slices to one side, standing up.
7. Add blackberries, raspberries, and strawberries.

SLICE SMART!
Hold the fruit tight but keep your hands back from the blade.

Brown-Butter
CARROTS

Serves 6 | 10 Minutes

INGREDIENTS

- 1 cup carrot chips
- ¼ cup water
- 4 tbsps. butter
- ½ tsp. honey
- ¼ tsp. nutmeg
- ¼ tsp. salt
- ¼ tsp. pepper
- 2 tsps. fresh dill, chopped

INSTRUCTIONS

1. Add carrots and water to a medium skillet and cook on medium for 5 minutes.
2. Add butter and cook for 5 minutes.
3. Add honey, nutmeg, salt, and pepper and cook for 3 minutes.
4. Add dill and cook 1 minute.

STEAM!
Cooking the carrots in water keeps them moist!

Elote Deviled
EGGS

Serves 6 | 20 Minutes

INGREDIENTS

- 12 eggs
- ⅓ cup mayo
- 1 tbsp. mustard
- ¼ tsp. salt
- ¼ cup frozen mixed corn
- 2 tsps. elote seasoning or 1 tbsp. chili powder

INSTRUCTIONS

1. Add eggs to pot and fill with water until it reaches 1 inch above eggs.
2. Let water boil, then remove the pot of eggs from heat and let stand for 13 minutes.
3. Drain eggs and run cool water over them.
4. Peel eggs and slice in half.
5. Mix egg yolks, mayo, mustard, and salt in a bowl or directly in a ziplock bag.
6. Cut the tip of the bag and pipe the filling into the egg halves.
7. Defrost corn in the microwave, then toast for 1 to 2 minutes in the toaster oven or skillet.
8. Sprinkle eggs with corn and elote seasoning and serve.

PIPE!
Using a ziplock bag makes it easy to pipe the filling into the eggs!

Tajin Watermelon
BITES

Serves 2 | 5 Minutes

INGREDIENTS

1 cup watermelon

1 lime

1 tbsp. tajin or chili powder

1 bunch mint

INSTRUCTIONS

1. Slice watermelon into 1-inch cubes.
2. Slice lime in half and squeeze onto each watermelon cube.
3. Sprinkle tajin on each cube.
4. Top with a slice of mint.

SQUEEZE!
Squeeze a little lime juice onto each watermelon cube!

BRUSCHETTA

Serves 6 | 15 Minutes

INGREDIENTS

3 tbsps. olive oil

1 baguette, cut into 1-inch slices

1 cup cherry tomatoes

1 tbsp. garlic

½ tsp. salt

2 tbsps. basil, chopped

INSTRUCTIONS

1. Drizzle 1 tablespoon olive oil over baguette slices and toast in toaster oven or conventional oven at 350°F for 5 minutes.
2. Dice cherry tomatoes into ¼-inch pieces.
3. Sauté tomatoes in 2 tablespoons olive oil and garlic for 3 minutes in a medium skillet on medium heat.
4. Remove from heat.
5. Add salt and basil and stir.
6. Spoon oil, salt, and basil mixture onto each slice of baguette and serve.

SPOON!
Use a large spoon to scoop up the tomatoes and pour onto each slice of baguette.

Parmesan
CRISPS

Serves 4 | 15 Minutes

INGREDIENTS

One 6-oz. bag shredded Parmesan (or cheese of your choice)

1 tbsp. garlic powder

1 tbsp. dried parsley

INSTRUCTIONS

1. Preheat oven to 400°F.
2. Add 2 tablespoons of Parmesan cheese in separate circles to a silicone- or parchment-lined baking sheet.
3. Pat down the cheese to make little circles.
4. Sprinkle each cheese circle with a pinch of garlic powder and dried parsley.
5. Bake for 5 minutes or until the edges are golden brown.

PINCH!
Use your fingers to pinch the cheese into circles!

Sautéed
VEGGIES

Serves 6 | 25 Minutes

INGREDIENTS

- 2 zucchini
- 2 yellow squash
- 3 tbsps. olive oil
- ½ onion, diced
- 1 tsp. turmeric
- 1 tbsp. chopped garlic
- 2 tbsps. liquid aminos (or soy sauce)

INSTRUCTIONS

1. Slice zucchini and squash into thin slices.
2. Add olive oil and onion to a pan and sauté on medium heat.
3. Add veggies to pan and cook 5 to 10 minutes.
4. Add turmeric, garlic, and liquid aminos. Cook an additional 10 minutes or until veggies are softened.

SLICE THIN!
These veggies taste really good when they are thinly sliced. Take your time and slice evenly.

Spam
MUSUBI 🍲 🚫

Serves 6 | 15 Minutes

INGREDIENTS

One 1-oz. package sushi nori seaweed

One 12-oz. can Spam

1 tbsp. brown sugar

2 tbsps. soy sauce

2 cups cooked white rice

INSTRUCTIONS

1. Slice sushi sheets into 2-inch-wide strips.
2. Slice Spam into ¼-inch pieces.
3. Add brown sugar and soy sauce to a bowl and stir to combine.
4. Dip Spam pieces into sauce and coat. Set pieces on a plate.
5. Cook Spam on medium heat in a medium skillet for about 3 minutes per side.
6. Place sushi sheets lengthwise and add a scoop of rice to each, in the opposite direction.
7. Place cooked Spam on top of the rice.
8. Dip fingers into water and wrap the sushi together to close.

DIP!
Keep a small bowl of water next to you to make it easier to dip your fingers in the water.

Creamy Mashed
POTATOES

Serves 6 | 50 Minutes

INGREDIENTS

- 4 lbs. potatoes
- 1 cup milk
- 4 oz. butter
- 4 oz. cream cheese
- 1 tsp. salt

INSTRUCTIONS

1. Peel potatoes with a potato peeler.
2. Dice into 1-inch cubes.
3. Place in a large stockpot and add water until it reaches an inch above the potatoes.
4. Cook on medium heat for 40 minutes.
5. Strain potatoes and add back to pot.
6. Pour in milk, butter, cream cheese, and salt.
7. Use a potato masher to mash potatoes and combine ingredients.

MASH!
Mash through all the potatoes with a potato masher to make really creamy mashed potatoes. You can also use a mixer to combine if you prefer.

Grilled Veggie
SKEWERS

Serves 6 | 20 Minutes

INGREDIENTS

1 red bell pepper

1 yellow bell pepper

1 green bell pepper

1 cup mushrooms

½ cup cherry tomatoes

1 tbsp. olive oil

1 tsp. salt

INSTRUCTIONS

1. Slice peppers down the sides, around the core. Slice into 1-inch chunks.
2. Use a paper towel to clean off mushroom tops. Pull mushroom stems off and discard. Slice mushroom tops in half.
3. Add veggies to bamboo skewers, alternating colors and veggies. Repeat until all veggies are used up.
4. Brush on olive oil and sprinkle with salt.
5. Grill at 350°F for 12 to 15 minutes, rotating every few minutes.

SING A SONG!
Red, yellow, green, tomato, mushroom. Red, yellow, green, tomato, mushroom! Singing a song while you make these skewers will help you remember the order you put the veggies on!

Potato
SALAD

Serves 4 | 15 Minutes

INGREDIENTS

- 15 small-to-medium red potatoes
- 3 eggs
- 15 dill pickle chips, or 3 pickle spears
- ¼ cup avocado mayo
- ½ cup sour cream
- 2 tbsps. pickle juice
- 2 tbsps. mustard
- Salt
- Pepper

INSTRUCTIONS

1. Peel and cube potatoes.
2. Simmer potatoes in water on medium heat until cooked through, 20 to 25 minutes.
3. Boil eggs, then peel and slice.
4. Chop pickles into small pieces.
5. Add all ingredients to a bowl. Gently stir until combined without mashing.

PICKLES!
Fresh-made or high-quality store-bought pickles are the best choice for this recipe!

Peanut Butter
POWER BALLS

Serves 4–6 | 5 minutes

INGREDIENTS

1 cup quick oats

2 tbsps. honey

1 tsp. cinnamon

1 cup peanut butter

½ cup chocolate chips

INSTRUCTIONS

1. Pour oats, honey, cinnamon, and peanut butter into a large mixing bowl and stir.
2. Stir in chocolate chips.
3. Use a 1-inch cookie scoop to separate into balls.
4. Roll each ball to round out.

STIR!
Stir slowly so the ingredients stay in the bowl!

Heavenly
POTATOES

Serves 4–6 | 50 Minutes

INGREDIENTS

- ½ yellow onion, diced
- 1 tbsp. olive oil
- One 8-oz. package cream cheese, softened
- One 16-oz. tub sour cream
- Salt and pepper, to taste
- One 30-oz. package frozen hash browns
- One 16-oz. package cooked chicken
- One 8-oz. package cheddar cheese
- Green onions, chopped, for garnish

INSTRUCTIONS

1. Preheat oven to 350°F.
2. Sauté onion in olive oil until cooked.
3. Add cream cheese and stir.
4. Add sour cream, salt, and pepper and stir. Remove from heat.
5. Pour hash browns and chicken into a 13 × 9-inch casserole dish.
6. Stir in cream mixture, then sprinkle the top with cheese.
7. Bake at 350°F for 40 minutes or until cheese is melted.
8. Garnish with chopped green onions.

COMBINE!
Combine all ingredients in the casserole dish to use fewer dishes!

Roasted Garlic
HUMMUS

Serves 6 | 35 Minutes

INGREDIENTS

1 head garlic

3 tbsps. olive oil

1 tsp. + sprinkle salt

1 lemon

One 15-oz. can garbanzo beans

2–3 tbsps. water

INSTRUCTIONS

1. Preheat toaster oven to 350°F.
2. Peel outer layer of garlic off. Slice tips off.
3. Place garlic on toaster oven tray. Drizzle with 1 tablespoon of olive oil and add a sprinkle of salt.
4. Bake for 30 minutes.
5. Let garlic cool, then squeeze the garlic cloves out of their skins, pushing from the bottom up. Set a few pieces of garlic aside for garnish.
6. Slice lemon in half and use a lemon squeezer to pour juice into the blender.
7. Pour garbanzo beans and remaining olive oil, salt, and garlic, then the water, into blender.
8. Pulse until smooth. Scrape into a dish using a spatula or wooden spoon.

PUSH!
Push your thumbs from the bottom of the garlic up to get all of the cloves out.

Mixed
NUTS

Serves 6 | 20 Minutes

INGREDIENTS

¼ tsp. sage

¼ tsp. thyme

¼ tsp. chili powder

½ tsp. salt

½ tsp. pepper

1 tbsp. brown sugar

2 tbsps. olive oil

1 cup cashews

1 cup peanuts

1 cup pecans

INSTRUCTIONS

1. Preheat oven to 350°F.
2. Add all spices to a medium-size bowl and stir.
3. Add in olive oil and stir.
4. Add in all nuts and stir.
5. Pour onto a parchment-lined baking sheet and bake for 10 minutes.

MEASURE!
Use your measuring utensils to notice the difference between ½ teaspoon, ¼ teaspoon, and 1 tablespoon.

Friday-Night
POPCORN

Serves 6 | 10 Minutes

INGREDIENTS

- ¼ tsp. celery seed
- ½ tsp. onion powder
- ¼ tsp. chili powder

- ½ tsp. granulated garlic
- ¼ tsp. coriander
- ¼ tsp. pepper

- 4 tbsps. butter
- 3 tbsps. coconut oil
- ½ cup popcorn kernels

INSTRUCTIONS

1. Add all seasonings to a small dish and stir.
2. Add butter to a microwave-safe dish and microwave for 30 seconds.
3. Add coconut oil and popcorn kernels to a medium stockpot on medium heat with lid slightly ajar.
4. Allow kernels to pop while occasionally shaking the pan.
5. Occasionally tip the lid away from you to let the steam out. Popcorn will be done when the popping slows down.
6. Pour half of the popcorn into a large bowl.
7. Add half of the melted butter and half of the seasoning into the large bowl and stir.
8. Add second half of the popcorn, remaining butter, and seasoning into the bowl and stir.
9. Pour all popcorn into the large bowl or small bowls to serve.

HALF AT A TIME!
Adding butter and seasoning to half of the popcorn at a time will ensure the popcorn is all seasoned well!

Cotija
CORN 🍲 🔪

INGREDIENTS

4–5 ears corn

¼ cup cotija cheese

½ lime, juiced

½ tsp. chili powder

¼ cup mayo

Salt and pepper, to taste

2 tbsps. cilantro, chopped, to garnish

INSTRUCTIONS

1. Preheat oven to 400°F.
2. Bake corn on a parchment-lined baking sheet for 10 minutes.
3. Cut cotija cheese into small pieces about the size of corn kernels.
4. Cut corn off the cob and pour into a bowl.
5. Stir in remaining ingredients and let chill.
6. Garnish with cilantro and serve.

CUT!
Set the corn on its side to cut. That way the kernels will stay on the cutting board.

Spanish
RICE

Serves 6-8 | 30 Minutes

INGREDIENTS

4 tbsps. olive oil

1 onion, diced

One 3-oz. package cooked bacon bits

2 cups white rice

Two 0.2-oz. packets sazón or 2 tbsps. tomato bouillon

4 cups chicken broth

½ cup salsa

INSTRUCTIONS

1. In a large skillet on medium heat, sauté onion and bacon in olive oil for about 5 minutes.
2. Add in rice and cook for 1 minute.
3. Add in sazón, chicken broth, and salsa and bring to a boil.
4. Reduce heat to low and simmer, covered, for 20 minutes.

BROTH!
Keep chicken bouillon cubes on hand in the spice cabinet so you can always make chicken broth. To create 1 cup of chicken broth, combine 1 cube with 1 cup of warm water. This recipe takes 4 cups of water and 4 cubes of bouillon.

Kids' Fav

MAIN DISHES

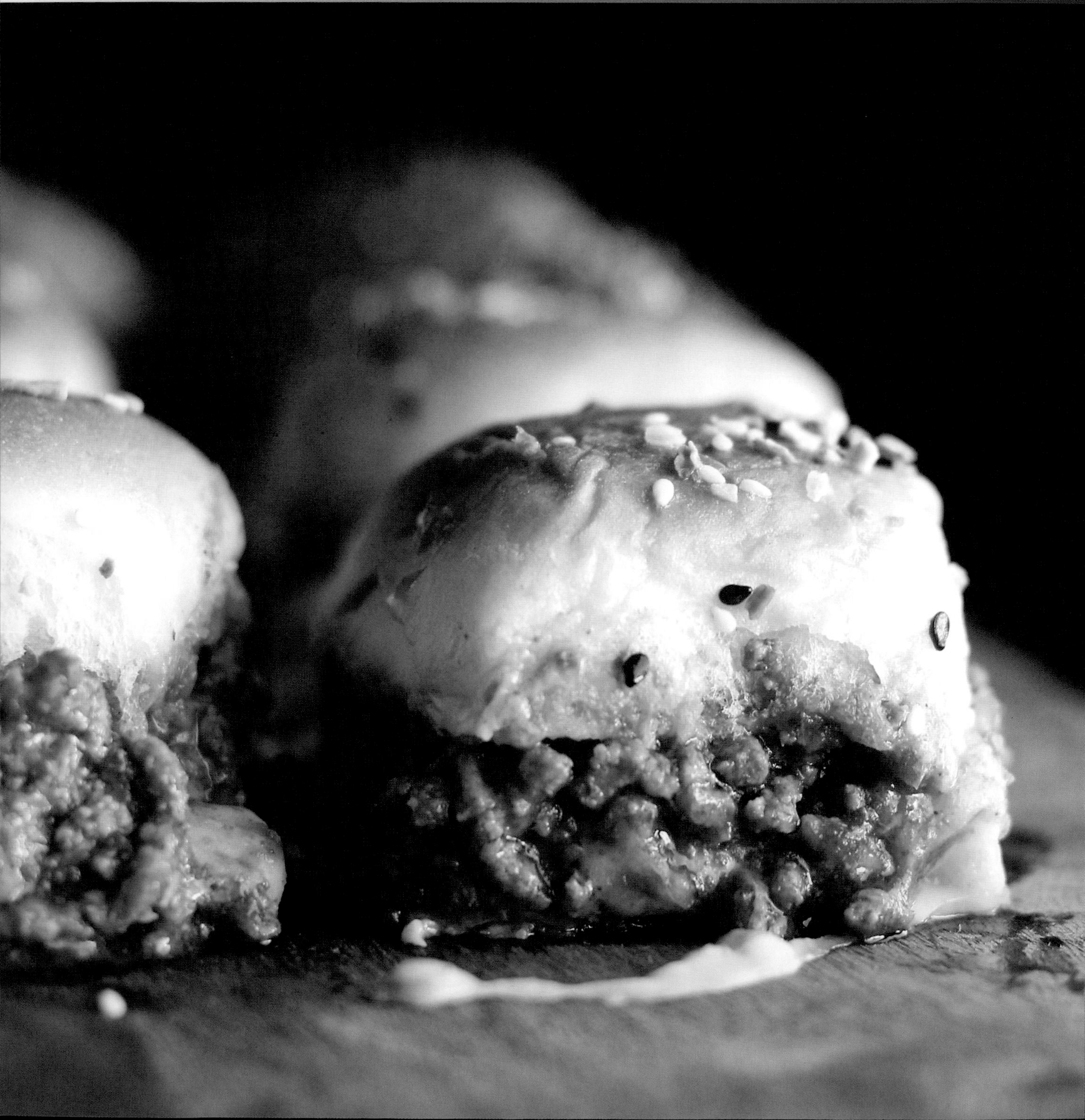

Mini Sloppy JOES

Serves 4–6 | 35 Minutes

INGREDIENTS

- 1 lb. ground beef
- One 15-oz. can sloppy joe sauce (I used Manwich)
- One 12-oz. package Hawaiian rolls
- One 8-oz. package sliced mozzarella cheese
- 2 tbsps. butter, melted
- 1 tbsp. everything bagel seasoning

INSTRUCTIONS

1. Sauté the ground beef in a skillet on medium heat until cooked through.
2. Add the Manwich sauce and simmer for 1 to 2 minutes.
3. Cut the Hawaiian rolls in half. Then add sliced mozzarella to the bottom halves.
4. Pour the sloppy joe mixture on top of the cheese.
5. Place the top halves of the Hawaiian rolls on top to complete the sandwiches.
6. Pour the melted butter on top of the sandwiches.
7. Sprinkle on the everything bagel seasoning.
8. Toast for 8 to 10 minutes in the toaster oven or conventional oven at 300°F.

SAY CHEESE!
Add the sliced cheese to the bottom of the sandwiches so the sloppy joe meat doesn't soak into the bread and make it *too* sloppy!

BBQ Chicken
DRUMSTICKS

Serves 4-6 | 1 Hour

INGREDIENTS

- 3 tbsps. carne asada seasoning
- One 3–5-lb. package chicken drumsticks
- 8-oz. barbecue sauce

INSTRUCTIONS

1. Start the barbecue grill.
2. While the barbecue is warming up, sprinkle a light, even coating of carne asada seasoning on all sides of the drumsticks.
3. Grill for about 45 minutes to 1 hour depending on the thickness of the chicken.
4. Make sure to rotate the chicken a quarter turn every 10 to 15 minutes to cook all sides evenly.
5. Pour barbecue sauce in a large bowl.
6. Use tongs to coat each piece of chicken evenly with the sauce.
7. Place each piece on a baking sheet or serving tray.

SEASON!
Sprinkle the seasoning evenly to get flavor on all of the pieces.

Avocado
SALAD ⊘

INGREDIENTS

3 avocados

1 corn on the cob

½ cucumber

½ lime, juiced

¼ tsp. salt

1 tbsp. chopped cilantro

INSTRUCTIONS

1. Slice avocados in half and scoop out with a spoon. Dice into ¼-inch pieces and place into a medium-size bowl.
2. Cut corn off the cob and add to bowl.
3. Dice cucumber into ¼-inch pieces and add to bowl.
4. Add remaining ingredients and stir gently to combine.

SCOOP!
Hold the avocado in one hand and use the spoon to scrape along the inside of the skin to scoop out. Cut around the pit or remove it if it comes out easily.

Spinach & Tomato
FLATBREAD

Serves 1–2 | 15 Minutes

INGREDIENTS

2 tbsps. garlic

2 tbsps. olive oil

10 cherry tomatoes, sliced

2 cups spinach

1 flatbread

¼ cup shredded cheese

INSTRUCTIONS

1. Sauté garlic in olive oil on medium heat for 1 minute.
2. Add tomatoes and cook until softened.
3. Add spinach and cook for 2 minutes.
4. Pour ingredients on top of flatbread.
5. Add flatbread to a foil-lined baking sheet for the toaster oven.
6. Toast at 350°F for 10 minutes.

SLICE!
Use a pizza cutter to slice the flatbread into triangles.

Cranberry Spinach
SALAD

Serves 4 | 5 Minutes

INGREDIENTS

4 tbsps. olive oil

2 tbsps. deli mustard

2 tbsps. honey

½ cup orange juice, fresh squeezed

1 avocado

2 tbsps. goat cheese

1 tbsp. everything bagel seasoning

One 10-oz. package spinach

2 tbsps. dried cranberries

2 tbsps. sliced almonds

INSTRUCTIONS

1. Whisk olive oil, mustard, honey, and orange juice together. Refrigerate until ready to use.
2. Slice avocados and crumble goat cheese.
3. Sprinkle everything bagel seasoning on avocados.
4. Add spinach to a bowl, pour on salad dressing, add goat cheese, avocado slices, cranberries, and almonds.

DRESS IT UP!
Double the recipe if you like extra dressing on your salads.

Easy Stovetop
MAC & CHEESE

Serves 6 | 25 Minutes

INGREDIENTS

- 1 lb. elbow macaroni
- ¼ cup butter
- 2 tbsps. flour
- 2 cups milk
- ½ tsp. salt
- ½ tsp. onion powder
- ¼ tsp. ground mustard
- ¼ tsp. garlic powder
- ¼ tsp. pepper
- 2 cups shredded sharp cheddar cheese
- 2 cups shredded mozzarella cheese

INSTRUCTIONS

1. Boil water and cook noodles according to package instructions.
2. Melt butter in a large skillet on medium heat.
3. Add flour and stir until thick.
4. Slowly add milk and stir until combined and thick.
5. Add seasonings and stir.
6. Add cheese and stir.
7. Drain noodles and combine with cheese sauce.

THICKEN!
Make sure all of the cheese melts and the sauce is thick.

Mongolian Beef
NOODLES

Serves 4 | 25 Minutes

INGREDIENTS

One 8–10-oz. package rice noodles

1 lb. ground beef

Salt and pepper, to taste

⅓ cup soy sauce

¼ cup granulated sugar

1 tbsp. maple syrup

1 tbsp. garlic

1 bunch green onions

Everything bagel seasoning (optional)

INSTRUCTIONS

1. Boil water and cook rice noodles for 10 minutes.
2. Brown ground beef on medium heat and season with salt and pepper.
3. In a medium bowl, combine soy sauce, sugar, maple syrup, and garlic. Whisk together.
4. Chop green onions.
5. Pour sauce into cooked ground beef and cook for 1 minute.
6. Stir in noodles.
7. Add to bowls, top with green onions, sprinkle with everything bagel seasoning, and serve.

SAUCE!
Make the sauce in a bowl to combine before adding to the meat.

Brats &
VEGGIES

Serves 6-8 | 1 Hour

INGREDIENTS

7 small red potatoes (or 2-3 russets)

1 bell pepper

Baby carrots (optional, can add extra veggies)

2-3 tbsps. olive oil

Salt, to taste

1 tbsp. chopped onion (raw or powder)

1 tbsp. garlic

7 bratwursts

INSTRUCTIONS

1. Preheat oven to 400°F.
2. Line sheet pan with parchment paper.
3. Slice potatoes and chop veggies.
4. Add olive oil, salt, chopped onion, and garlic to the veggies and combine.
5. Add brats in between veggies.
6. Cook for 40 to 50 minutes.

SPACE THEM OUT!
Give the brats space to cook. Spread them evenly around the pan, with the veggies in between.

Chicken ENCHILADAS

Serves 6–8 | 40 Minutes

INGREDIENTS

- 1 tbsp. olive oil
- 1 chopped yellow onion
- 1 lb. chicken breast strips

- ¼ cup water
- One 8-oz. package cream cheese
- One 28-oz. can red enchilada sauce

- 10 tortillas
- ½ cup shredded cheddar cheese
- One 4-oz. can diced green chilies

INSTRUCTIONS

1. Preheat oven to 350°F.
2. Sauté onion in olive oil for 2 minutes on medium heat.
3. Add chicken and water and cook chicken for 5 minutes on each side, then drain any excess water.
4. Add cream cheese and stir until combined, then remove from heat.
5. Pour 2 tablespoons of enchilada sauce in 13 × 9-inch baking dish and spread evenly.
6. Shred chicken with a fork.
7. Add chicken and cream cheese filling to tortillas and roll up.
8. Add each rolled-up tortilla to baking dish until the dish is full.
9. Top with remaining enchilada sauce and sprinkle cheddar cheese and green chilies on top.
10. Bake for 25 minutes.

FILLING!
Scoop about a half of a cup of filling into each tortilla.

Pasta
ALFREDO

Serves 4 | 15 Minutes

INGREDIENTS

½ cup butter

1 tbsp. flour

1 pint heavy cream

1 cup fresh Parmesan cheese, grated

One 16-oz. package fettuccine noodles, cooked

1 bunch broccoli, chopped

½ tsp. salt

½ tsp. pepper

INSTRUCTIONS

1. Melt butter.
2. Add flour until combined.
3. Add cream and simmer for 8 minutes stirring occasionally.
4. Stir in Parmesan cheese and seasonings and simmer for 2 to 3 minutes.
5. Add to noodles or veggies and serve.

THICKEN!
Your Alfredo sauce will thicken as you cook it slowly.

California Turkey
BOWLS

Serves 6–8 | 40 Minutes

INGREDIENTS

1 cup rice

1 lb. organic ground turkey

1 tbsp. taco seasoning + 2 tbsps. water

Avocado, sliced

Tomatoes, sliced

Mini bell peppers, sliced

One 15-oz. can black beans

1 lime

½ jalapeño, chopped (optional)

¼ cup ranch dressing

1 head romaine lettuce, chopped

½ cup shredded cheese

Chopped cilantro

INSTRUCTIONS

1. Cook rice according to package directions.
2. Brown ground turkey on medium heat until cooked through.
3. Add taco seasoning and water to turkey and let simmer for 5 minutes.
4. Chop/slice all veggies and set aside.
5. Heat up beans and set aside.
6. Add lime juice and jalapeño to ranch to make jalapeño ranch sauce.
7. Add chopped lettuce to cover bottom of bowl.
8. In layers, add turkey, black beans, rice, veggies, and cheese. Top with jalapeño ranch sauce and garnish with cilantro.

GET CREATIVE!
You pick which toppings you'd like each time you cook this.

Baked Chicken
FLAUTAS

Serves 4 | 20 Minutes

INGREDIENTS

- 1 cup leftover or shredded chicken
- 1 cup shredded cheddar cheese
- ½ cup cream cheese
- ½ cup mashed potatoes
- 1 tbsp. chopped cilantro
- 6 tortillas
- 2 tbsps. olive oil
- Sour cream, salsa, and chopped cilantro for garnish

INSTRUCTIONS

1. Preheat oven to 400°F.
2. Mix chicken, cheese, cream cheese, potatoes, and cilantro in a bowl.
3. Add 2 tablespoons of the mixture into each tortilla and roll up.
4. Drizzle olive oil on a baking sheet.
5. Place all rolled-up tortillas on the baking sheet, touching so they don't unravel. Drizzle with remaining olive oil.
6. Bake for 8 to 10 minutes or until edges brown.
7. Garnish with sour cream, salsa, and cilantro.

ROLL!
Roll up tortillas and push them together so they don't come undone.

Turkey Lettuce CUPS

Serves 4-5 | 35 Minutes

INGREDIENTS

- 1 lb. ground turkey
- 3–4 tbsps. soyaki sauce
- 1 yellow or white onion, chopped
- 1 cucumber
- 1–2 bell peppers
- 10 cherry tomatoes
- ¼ cup carrots
- 3 tbsps. olive oil
- Salt, to taste
- 1 head romaine lettuce
- 1 cup cooked white rice

INSTRUCTIONS

1. Cook turkey on medium heat in a large skillet until lightly browned.
2. Add soyaki to meat, set aside.
3. Chop all veggies into ½-inch pieces.
4. Sauté onion with olive oil and salt, set aside.
5. Cut romaine lettuce to palm-size cups.
6. Top lettuce with rice, turkey, caramelized onions, and veggies.

CHOP!
Chop all veggies into small, bite-size pieces, about ½ inch long.

Kids' Fav
CHILI

Serves 6 | 40 Minutes

INGREDIENTS

½ onion, chopped

2 tbsps. olive oil

1 lb. ground sausage

2 tbsps. chili powder

1 tbsp. cumin

½ tsp. salt + ½ tsp. pepper

One 15-oz. can kidney beans, drained

One 15-oz. can white beans, drained

One 32-oz. can crushed tomatoes

INSTRUCTIONS

1. Sauté onions in olive oil until translucent, 3 minutes.
2. Add sausage and seasonings and cook through, 12 minutes.
3. Add remaining ingredients and simmer for 20 minutes.

SQUEEZE!
Squeeze the can opener tight, and turn until open!

Tortilla
SOUP

Serves 4–6 | 20 Minutes

INGREDIENTS

One 15-oz. can corn

One 15-oz. can black beans

One 12.5-oz. can cooked chicken

One 15-oz. can fire-roasted tomatoes

One 15-oz. jar salsa

One 32-oz. box chicken stock

1 tbsp. garlic

1 tbsp. cumin

1 tbsp. chili powder

Lime, avocado, cilantro, shredded cheese, tortilla strips (optional)

INSTRUCTIONS

1. Open all cans, salsa, and stock and pour into a stockpot and heat on medium heat.
2. Add garlic, cumin, and chili powder and simmer for 20 minutes.
3. Add optional toppings to each dish as desired.

POUR!
Pour cans slowly so they don't splash out of the stockpot.

Bacon & Cheddar
BURGERS

Serves 4 | 20 minutes

INGREDIENTS

1 lb. ground beef

4 slices cheddar cheese

One 2.5-oz. package cooked bacon

1 tsp. garlic salt

1 tsp. pepper

INSTRUCTIONS

1. Place ground beef in bowl.
2. Slice cheddar and bacon into ½-inch square pieces.
3. Pour cheddar, bacon, and seasoning into the bowl. Stir to combine.
4. Press into 4 burger patties with your hands.
5. Grill on medium to low heat for 5 to 7 minutes per side.

PRESS!
Press the meat into patties with your hands! Mash ingredients together and shape into a flat circle about ½ inch thick. When transferring to the grill, use parchment paper to keep the patties separated.

Shrimp
SKEWERS

Serves 4 | 20 Minutes

INGREDIENTS

One 32-oz. bag frozen shrimp

1 tsp. granulated garlic

¼ tsp. pepper

¼ tsp. cumin

¼ tsp. chili powder

1 pinch salt

¼ cup butter, melted

INSTRUCTIONS

1. Defrost shrimp in a strainer set in a bowl of cold water.
2. Add all seasoning into a large bowl.
3. Pour in melted butter and stir.
4. Add in defrosted shrimp and stir.
5. Add 4 to 6 shrimps onto a bamboo skewer, so they lay flat.
6. Grill at 300°F for 2 to 3 minutes per side.

STRAIN!
Use a strainer to defrost the shrimp. That way, the shrimp can be pulled right out of the water and poured into the seasonings.

Chicken Salad
SAMMIES

Serves 6 | 40 Minutes

INGREDIENTS

4 chicken breasts

1 cup grapes

2 stalks celery

½ tsp. salt

¼ tsp. pepper

2 tsps. Dijon mustard

½ cup mayo

INSTRUCTIONS

1. Boil large pot of water, add chicken breast, and cook for 20 minutes.
2. Slice grapes into quarters.
3. Slice celery into thin pieces.
4. Once chicken is cooked, cut into small pieces.
5. Add all ingredients into a mixing bowl and stir.
6. Add chicken salad to plain or toasted bread.

MIX!
Mix all the ingredients together!

Chicken
QUESADILLAS

Serves 1-2 | 10 Minutes

INGREDIENTS

- 1 chicken breast, cooked
- 2 tbsps. barbecue sauce
- 2 tsps. butter
- 2 tortillas
- ½ cup cheese
- 1 tbsp. ranch dressing

INSTRUCTIONS

1. Heat up chicken on a griddle pan on medium heat.
2. Spread 1 tablespoon of barbecue sauce on the chicken.
3. Take chicken out of the pan and cut into pieces.
4. Butter one side of each tortilla.
5. Lay one tortilla butter side down in the griddle pan. Top with shredded cheese and chicken.
6. Add second tortilla to the top, butter side up.
7. Cook until cheese starts to melt.
8. Flip with a spatula and grill on second side until cheese is completely melted and you can see grill marks.
9. Take out of the pan and slice into 8 pieces.
10. Drizzle on barbecue sauce and ranch dressing as desired and serve.

ADD SAUCE!
Add barbecue sauce to chicken before heating or while it's in the griddle pan.

Chicken
TENDERS

Serves 4 | 25 Minutes

INGREDIENTS

½ cup cream

1 egg

½ cup breadcrumbs

1 tsp. garlic-salt blend

½ tsp. carne asada seasoning

1-lb. package chicken tenders

3 tbsps. olive oil

INSTRUCTIONS

1. Set out two shallow dishes of equal size. Add cream and egg to one dish and stir.
2. Add breadcrumbs and seasonings to second dish and stir.
3. Use a fork to dip each chicken tender into the cream mixture and then into the breadcrumb mixture, coating evenly. Do this twice per piece of chicken and set aside on a plate.
4. Add olive oil to medium skillet pan and cook on medium heat.
5. Add all pieces of chicken to the pan and cook for 8 to 10 minutes per side.

COAT!
Using a fork to dip the chicken tenders keeps your fingers clean!

Lemon-Baked
FISH

Serves 6 | 35 Minutes

INGREDIENTS

1 lb. tilapia or white fish

½ cup melted butter

1 tbsp. minced garlic

1 tsp. carne asada seasoning

2 lemons, 1 sliced, 1 cut in half

2 tbsps. cilantro, chopped

INSTRUCTIONS

1. Preheat oven to 350°F.
2. Place fish into a 9-inch round baking dish, spreading it around in a circle. A little bit of overlap is okay.
3. Mix butter, garlic, and seasoning and squeeze half a lemon in a 2-cup liquid measuring cup. Pour onto fish, coating evenly.
4. Top with sliced lemons and cover with foil.
5. Bake for 25 minutes.
6. Garnish with cilantro and serve.

POUR ON THE YUM!
Top with lemons!

Philly ROLLS

Serves 4 | 10 minutes

INGREDIENTS

1 English cucumber

4 sheets seaweed

1 cup cooked rice

4 oz. cream cheese

4 oz. smoked salmon

INSTRUCTIONS

1. Slice cucumber into sticks. Cut lengthwise in half until you have ¼-inch sticks.
2. Lay out a sheet of seaweed on bamboo sushi mat or cutting board. Press ¼ cup of rice into sheet.
3. Add cream cheese, salmon, and cucumber to the middle of the rice-topped seaweed. Make sure ingredients are evenly laid out in the middle, from left to right.
4. Roll from the bottom up with your bamboo sushi mat, or use your fingers to tightly roll until edges of the seaweed meet.
5. Slice into ½-inch pieces.
6. Repeat for remaining rolls.

ROLL!
Roll the seaweed sheets from the bottom up and squeeze tight!

Pork + RICE

Serves 4 | 30 Minutes

INGREDIENTS

- 1 lb. pork cutlets
- 1 tsp. garlic salt
- 1 tsp. pepper
- 2 tbsps. olive oil
- 1 cup rice
- 1 tbsp. minced garlic
- 2 ¼ cups chicken broth
- 2 tbsps. chopped cilantro

INSTRUCTIONS

1. Sprinkle pork with seasoning.
2. Set electric pressure cooker to sauté and add olive oil.
3. Sauté pork for 3 minutes on each side. Turn sauté setting off.
4. Add rice, garlic, and chicken broth. Set electric pressure cooker to manual for 20 minutes.
5. Release electric pressure cooker with help from an adult.
6. Top with cilantro and serve.

POUR!
Pour the ingredients slowly into your electric pressure cooker and watch it all come together!

Sweets &
TREATS

Coconut Fudge
POPS

Serves 15 | 10 Minutes Prep | 1 Hour Freeze

INGREDIENTS

One 15-oz. can coconut milk

1 cup chocolate chips

1 bag popsicle sticks

INSTRUCTIONS

1. Pour ingredients into saucepan and melt on low-medium heat for 5 minutes or until ingredients combine.
2. Pour into a 2-cup liquid measuring cup.
3. Pour into ice tray. Freeze for 40 minutes.
4. Add 1 popsicle stick to each cube.
5. Freeze 20 minutes more and enjoy!

POUR!
Pour the mixture slowly into each ice cube spot to get even pops!

Candy Cane
DANISH

INGREDIENTS

4-oz. cream cheese

4 tbsps. powdered sugar

One 8-oz. can crescent roll dough

4 tbsps. strawberry jelly

1–1½ tbsps. milk

INSTRUCTIONS

1. Preheat oven to 375°F.
2. To make the filling, combine cream cheese and 2 tablespoons of powdered sugar.
3. Roll out the crescent dough on a silicone-lined cookie sheet.
4. Place triangle dough with the point of the triangle to the left, and overlap the pieces.
5. Press overlapping pieces together, starting at the bottom of the cookie sheet and working your way up. Once you get toward the top, start to turn the pieces to form the candy cane shape.
6. Add a spoonful of filling and jam to each triangle.
7. Wrap the pointed part of the triangle over the filling and press into dough.
8. Pinch the dough together on the sides so the filling stays inside.
9. Bake for 10 to 11 minutes, or until edges are lightly golden brown.
10. To make the icing, combine the remaining powdered sugar with milk.
11. Drizzle icing on the candy cane Danish. Enjoy!

WRAP!
Wrap the small edge of the triangle over the filling to press into the opposite side of the dough.

Brown-Butter COOKIES

Serves 8 | 20 Minutes

INGREDIENTS

- 1¾ cups flour
- ¾ tsp. baking soda
- ¾ tsp. baking powder
- ½ tsp. salt

- 1 cup unsalted butter, room temperature
- ½ cup brown sugar
- ¼ cup granulated sugar
- 1 egg

- ½ tsp. vanilla
- 1 cup 70% cocoa baking chocolate, chopped
- 1 tsp. salt, for finishing

INSTRUCTIONS

1. Preheat oven to 375°F.
2. Combine flour, baking soda, baking powder, and salt in a bowl.
3. Brown a ½ cup of butter in a skillet by melting until it bubbles. Turn off the heat after it bubbles for about 30 seconds so it doesn't burn. Then place in a dish in freezer to chill.
4. In a stand-mixer bowl, combine remaining butter with brown sugar and granulated sugar. Mix using paddle attachment.
5. Add in egg until combined. Add in vanilla and browned butter.
6. Add in flour mixture until just mixed.
7. Stir in the chopped chocolate.
8. Bake for 9 minutes or until bottom edges look brown.
9. Sprinkle finishing salt on top.

SPRINKLE!
Sprinkle finishing salt on top of cookies when they are fresh out of the oven!

Star-Spangled COOKIES

Serves 8 | 30 Minutes

INGREDIENTS

1 cup unsalted butter, softened

1 cup granulated sugar

1 egg

2 tsps. vanilla extract

1 tsp. salt

3 cups all-purpose flour

One 8-oz. package cream cheese, softened

2 tbsps. powdered sugar

One 1-lb. package strawberries

One 6-oz. package blueberries

INSTRUCTIONS

1. Preheat oven to 350°F.
2. Combine butter and sugar in stand-mixer bowl. Add egg, vanilla, and salt and combine.
3. Add flour until combined. Refrigerate mixture for 10 minutes.
4. Roll out dough on a floured surface. Use a star cookie cutter to cut out cookies, then place on baking sheet.
5. Bake for 10 minutes and let cool.
6. While cookies are baking, mix the cream cheese and powdered sugar together and slice the strawberries into sixths.
7. Spread the cream cheese mixture onto the cooled cookies.
8. Place the sliced strawberries on each point, with one blueberry in the center.

PRESS!
Press the cookie cutter into the dough so it goes all the way to the cutting board. Wiggle slightly to separate the shape from the dough.

Cranberry COOKIES

Serves 6 | 30 Minutes

INGREDIENTS

1 cup granulated sugar

1 cup water

One 12-oz. package cranberries

½ cup raspberries

1 tbsp. lemon zest

1 package sugar cookie dough

INSTRUCTIONS

Cranberry Sauce:

1. Add sugar and water to a saucepan and simmer until combined.
2. Add cranberries and raspberries and simmer 10 to 15 minutes.
3. Add lemon zest and stir.
4. Refrigerate for 15 minutes.

Cookies:

1. Preheat oven to 350°F.
2. Place cookies on ungreased cookie sheet and bake for 14 minutes.
3. Right as cookies come out of the oven, use the handle of a wooden spoon to press a circle into the center of each cookie.
4. Add ½ teaspoon of cranberry sauce to center of each cookie.
5. Top with additional cranberry sauce and coconut flakes as desired. You will have cranberry sauce left over to enjoy as you please.

PRESS!
It's easiest to press the cookies when they're fresh out of the oven.

Blueberries & Cream
GALETTES

Serves 6 | 30 Minutes

INGREDIENTS

1 box frozen puff pastry shells

1 cup blueberries

1 tbsp. granulated sugar

4 oz. cream cheese

½ cup powdered sugar

1 cup whipping cream

INSTRUCTIONS

1. Preheat oven to 425°F.
2. Place pastry shells on a parchment-lined cookie sheet and bake for 18 to 20 minutes. Let cool on a wire rack.
3. Add blueberries and granulated sugar to a medium saucepan and heat for 5 to 7 minutes on medium heat, stirring occasionally. Then set blueberries on a pot holder in the refrigerator to cool.
4. Add cream cheese to stand mixer and mix for 3 minutes on low.
5. Add powdered sugar to cream cheese and mix for 2 minutes on low.
6. Add whipping cream to cream cheese and mix for 5 minutes, or until fluffy.
7. Fill pastry shells with whipped cream cheese mixture and pour blueberry sauce on top. Add more whipped cream cheese mixture on top of the blueberries. You may have additional blueberry sauce left over for dipping.

SQUEEZE!
Put a large ziplock bag in a large cup. Use a spatula to put the whipped cream cheese into the bag. Cut a ½-inch tip off the point of the bag. Squeeze the bag to add the whipped cream cheese to the pastry shells.

Lemon Crinkle
COOKIES

Serves 8 | 30 Minutes

INGREDIENTS

- 2 cups flour
- ½ tsp. salt
- 1½ tsp. baking powder

- ½ cup butter, room temperature
- 1 cup granulated sugar
- 1 lemon

- 2 eggs, room temperature
- ½ tsp. vanilla extract
- ½ cup powdered sugar

INSTRUCTIONS

1. Preheat oven to 350°F.
2. Combine flour, salt, and baking powder in a large bowl and set aside.
3. In stand-mixer bowl, cream butter and granulated sugar together until fluffy.
4. Zest lemon and add to sugar mixture and combine.
5. Add the eggs one at a time while stirring on low.
6. Juice the lemon and add to mixture, then add vanilla until combined.
7. Slowly add the flour mixture until combined.
8. Add powdered sugar to a small bowl.
9. Use a cookie scoop to roll the dough into ½-inch balls and roll each ball in powdered sugar until covered.
10. Arrange cookies 2 inches apart on parchment-lined baking sheet and bake for about 12 minutes.

ROLL!
Roll the dough balls in the powdered sugar until covered on all sides.

Peanut Butter Cup
CUPCAKES

Serves 12 | 35 Minutes

INGREDIENTS

For the Cupcakes:
- 1 cup granulated sugar
- ½ cup butter
- 2 eggs
- 2 tsps. vanilla extract
- 1½ cups all-purpose flour
- 1¾ tsps. baking powder
- ½ cup milk
- ¼ cup peanut butter
- 18 mini peanut butter cups

For the Icing:
- 1 cup butter
- 3½ cups powdered sugar
- 1½ tsps. vanilla extract
- ¼ cup milk
- ¼ cup peanut butter
- ¼ cup cocoa powder

INSTRUCTIONS

For the Cupcakes:
1. Preheat oven to 350°F.
2. Line a muffin pan with paper liners.
3. In a medium bowl, cream together the granulated sugar and butter.
4. Beat in the eggs, one at a time, and stir in the vanilla.
5. Combine flour and baking powder, add to the creamed mixture, and mix well.
6. Stir in milk until batter is smooth, then mix in peanut butter.
7. Pour or spoon batter a quarter of the way into the prepared pan.
8. Add 1 peanut butter cup to each cupcake. Cut remaining peanut butter cups in half to decorate the top of the cupcake after frosting.
9. Pour or spoon remaining batter on top of peanut butter cups to cover, until pan is about three-quarters full.
10. Bake for 20 to 25 minutes.

For the Icing:
1. Beat butter until fluffy.
2. Add sugar and beat for about 3 more minutes.
3. Add the vanilla and milk and beat for another 6 minutes until fluffy.
4. Add peanut butter and cocoa powder and mix until combined.
5. Scoop icing into a large ziplock bag. Cut a ¼-inch hole in the tip of the bag. Squeeze the bag to frost the cupcakes.
6. Top the cupcake with a half-piece of peanut butter cup.

DROP! Put a peanut butter cup into the center of each cupcake!

Chocolate
PARTY MIX

Serves 6 | 5 Minutes

INGREDIENTS

- 3 cups popped popcorn
- 3 cups square rice cereal (I used Rice Chex)
- ½ cup peanuts
- 1 cup peanut butter pretzels
- ½ cup chocolate chips
- 2 tbsps. butter, melted
- ½ tsp. cinnamon
- 1 tsp. brown sugar

INSTRUCTIONS

1. Mix popcorn, cereal, peanuts, pretzels, and chocolate in a medium-size microwavable bowl.
2. Mix butter, cinnamon, and brown sugar in a small dish.
3. Pour the butter mixture onto the cereal mixture and stir.
4. Microwave for 30 seconds.
5. Stir again and enjoy!

STIR!
Use your measuring spoon to stir for fewer dishes.

Holiday Monster COOKIES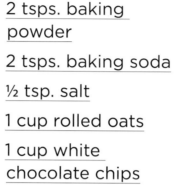

Serves 6 | 25 Minutes

INGREDIENTS

- 2 sticks butter
- 1 cup brown sugar
- ½ cup granulated sugar
- 2 tbsps. vanilla
- 2 eggs
- 2 cups flour

- 2 tsps. baking powder
- 2 tsps. baking soda
- ½ tsp. salt
- 1 cup rolled oats
- 1 cup white chocolate chips

- 1 cup mini chocolate chips
- 1 cup pretzels, crushed in bite-size pieces
- 1 cup mini M&M's

INSTRUCTIONS

1. Preheat oven to 350°F.
2. Add butter, brown sugar, and granulated sugar to stand-mixer bowl and combine with paddle attachment for 2 to 3 minutes.
3. Add vanilla and eggs and combine for 1 minute.
4. Add flour, baking powder, baking soda, and salt to a large bowl and stir.
5. Add flour mixture into butter mixture and combine.
6. Add in oats and combine.
7. Stir in white chocolate chips, mini chocolate chips, pretzels, and mini M&M's.
8. Use a 1-inch cookie scoop to place cookie dough onto parchment paper- or silicone-lined cookie sheet.
9. Bake for 10 minutes or until edges are golden brown.

CRUNCH!
Pour pretzels into a plastic bag and crunch with your hands to make bite-size pieces.

Mint-Lemonade
POPSICLES

Serves 10 | 10 Minutes Prep | 6 Hours Freeze

INGREDIENTS

5 cups water

1 cup granulated sugar

4 lemons

½ cup mint

INSTRUCTIONS

1. Make a simple syrup by boiling the sugar in 1 cup of water in a small saucepan on medium heat.
2. Squeeze lemons into a blender and add mint. Blend mint and lemon juice for 1 minute.
3. Strain lemon-mint juice into a pitcher.
4. Pour simple syrup into the pitcher with remaining water and stir.
5. Pour into popsicle molds and freeze for 6 hours.

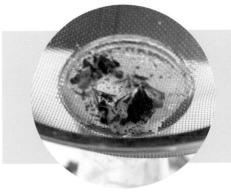

STRAIN!
Strain the mint out of the lemon juice after blending to keep mint leaves out of the popsicles!

Easy Christmas
COOKIES

Serves 6 | 25 Minutes

INGREDIENTS

1 package sugar cookie dough

½ cup flour

1 package cream cheese frosting

Assorted sprinkles, mini chocolate chips, or M&M's

INSTRUCTIONS

1. Preheat oven to 350°F.
2. On a floured surface, knead flour into dough.
3. Roll out dough ¼ inch thick.
4. Use cookie cutters to create shapes. Repeat until all dough is used.
5. Bake for 11 to 14 minutes.
6. Using a butter knife, spread frosting on each cookie and decorate with toppings.

FLOUR!
If your cookie cutters get sticky with dough, add some flour before pressing into the dough.

TIRAMISU

Serves 6-9 | 10 Minutes Prep | 4 Hours Rest

INGREDIENTS

1 cup mascarpone

¼ cup granulated sugar

1 tsp. vanilla

1 cup whipped cream

1 tsp. instant decaf coffee

1 cup hot water

One 12-oz. package chocolate- and vanilla-flavored ladyfinger cookies

1 tbsp. cocoa powder

INSTRUCTIONS

1. Add mascarpone, sugar, and vanilla into stand-mixer bowl and whip until combined.
2. Add whipped cream and mix on low.
3. Add coffee to hot water and pour into a bowl or dish.
4. Dip each ladyfinger into the coffee.
5. Place each cookie into an 8 × 8-inch dish to start the first layer. Add half of the cream mixture on top of the cookies.
6. Sprinkle half of the cocoa powder with a sifter onto the cream mixture.
7. Repeat, adding another layer of dipped cookies, then cream mixture, then cocoa powder.
8. Refrigerate for 4 hours before serving.

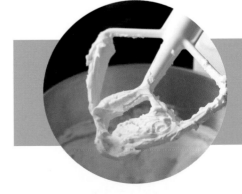

CREAM!
Make sure all cream is combined until it has a thick consistency.

Lemon Cheesecake
BITES

Serves 10 | 10 Minutes Prep | 4 Hours Chill

INGREDIENTS

8 oz. cream cheese, room temperature

½ cup powdered sugar

1 tsp. vanilla

1 tbsp. lemon juice

½ cup sour cream

1 cup whipped cream

12 thin lemon cookies

Zest of 1 lemon

INSTRUCTIONS

1. Add cream cheese and powdered sugar to a stand-mixer bowl and combine.
2. Add vanilla, lemon juice, and sour cream and mix on low.
3. Add whipped cream and combine on low.
4. Place 1 cookie in each spot in a cupcake pan.
5. Using 1-inch cookie scoop, add scoop of cheesecake mixture to each cookie.
6. Sprinkle on lemon zest.
7. Place in the refrigerator to chill for 4 hours.
8. Use a butter knife to tilt the cookies out of the pan and place on a serving plate.

SCOOP!
The cookie scoop will help create even bites!

Pumpkin Cider
POPSICLES ⊘

Serves 6 | 5 Minutes Prep | 6 Hours Freeze

INGREDIENTS

1 pear

1 banana

1 cup pumpkin apple cider

INSTRUCTIONS

1. Using potato peeler, peel skin off pear.
2. Chop pear and banana into 1-inch pieces.
3. Add all ingredients to blender and pulse until smooth.
4. Pour mixture into popsicle molds and freeze for 6 hours.

WARM THEM UP!
Run the popsicle molds under warm water to release popsicles easily.

Cookie
DOUGH

INGREDIENTS

1 cup flour

8 tbsps. butter, room temperature

1 cup brown sugar

2 tbsps. milk

1 tsp. vanilla

½ tsp. salt

½ cup mini chocolate chips

INSTRUCTIONS

1. Heat treat the flour so it is edible: Pour flour into a large glass bowl and microwave, in 30-second intervals, until it reaches 165°F. To check the internal temperature of the flour, use a candy thermometer. (You'll probably need to microwave the flour three times.)
2. Add butter and brown sugar to a stand-mixer bowl and mix until combined.
3. Add in milk, vanilla, and salt and mix until combined.
4. Slowly mix in flour until combined.
5. Remove dough from mixer and stir in chocolate chips.
6. Enjoy right away, or store in the refrigerator for up to 1 week. Edible cookie dough can also be stored in an airtight container in the freezer.

TASTE RIGHT AWAY!
Have a bite on a spoon or roll into bite-size balls after refrigerating for 20 minutes.

Chocolate Raspberry
TART

Serves 6 | 30 Minutes

INGREDIENTS

10 graham crackers

¼ tsp. salt

6 tbsps. butter, melted

Two 6-oz. packages raspberries

2 tbsps. granulated sugar

12 oz. semisweet chocolate

1 cup heavy cream

INSTRUCTIONS

1. Preheat oven to 350°F.
2. Pulse graham crackers, salt, and butter in blender until combined.
3. Push graham-cracker crust into a tart pan with the back of a measuring cup until even. Bake for 10 minutes.
4. Sauté 1 package of raspberries with sugar on medium heat until combined, about 3 minutes.
5. Pour chocolate and heavy cream into a microwave-safe bowl and melt for 30 seconds. Stir to combine.
6. Pour raspberry sauce onto cooked crust, evenly.
7. Pour chocolate sauce on top of raspberry sauce, evenly. Use a spatula to even edges.
8. Refrigerate for 15 minutes to set chocolate.
9. Decorate the tart with the remaining raspberries.

PUSH!
Push the crust into the pan!

Index

About the Author

BRIANNE GRAJKOWSKI is a popular food and lifestyle blogger behind the site www.BriGeeski.com. A mom of two who is known for creating fun and easy recipes she makes with her kids, Brianne is also an artist, creative entrepreneur, graphic designer, and adventure seeker who shares everyday recipes, travel ideas, things to do in San Diego, and life as a mompreneur. To learn more about Brianne, visit her website or follow her on social media (@BriGeeski).